Bug Patrol

LOOKING FOR ANTS

Written by

EMILIE DUFRESNE

KidHaven PUBLISHING

Published in 2023 by KidHaven Publishing,
an Imprint of Greenhaven Publishing, LLC
29 East 21st Street
New York, NY 10010

Edited by:
Madeline Tyler

Designed by:
Brandon Mattless

Cataloging-in-Publication Data

Names: Dufresne, Emilie.
Title: Looking for ants / Emilie Dufresne.
Description: New York : KidHaven Publishing, 2023. | Series: Bug patrol | Includes glossary and index.
Identifiers: ISBN 9781534541139 (pbk.) | ISBN 9781534541153 (library bound) ISBN 9781534541146 (6 pack) | ISBN 9781534541160 (ebook)
Subjects: LCSH: Ants--Juvenile literature.
Classification: LCC QL568.F7 D84 2023 | DDC 595.79'6--dc23

Manufactured in the United States of America

CPSIA compliance information: Batch #CSKH23: For further information contact Greenhaven Publishing LLC, New York, New York at 1-844-317-7404.

Please visit our website, www.greenhavenpublishing.com.
For a free color catalog of all our high-quality books,
call toll free 1-844-317-7404 or fax 1-844-317-7405.

Photo Credits

All images are courtesy of Shutterstock.com, unless otherwise specified. With thanks to Getty Images, Thinkstock Photo and iStockphoto. Front Cover – Africa Studio, Andrey Pavlov, Mehmet Doruk Tasci, rangizzz, Valentyn Volkov, musicman, artproem. Recurring Images – Andrey Pavlov, rangizzz, Valentyn Volkov, musicman, artproem, Filip Dokladal, Paladin12. 4–5 – Egor Kunovsky, Andrew Angelov. 6–7 – aaabbbccc, KK Tan, Olena Zaskochenko, PERLA BERANT WILDER, Yashkin Ilya. 8–9 – AG-PHOTOS, Panya_Anakotmankong, 10–11 – MacroPhotographyBD, PHOTO FUN, schankz. 12–13 – Gillian Pullinger, Hamik, Rainer Fuhrmann. 14–15 – Andrey Pavlov, ArtLovePhoto, xpixel. 16–17 – D. Kucharski K. Kucharska, Kevin Wells Photography, Salparadis. 18–19 – Patrick K. Campbell, SIN1980. 20–21 – Charles Andrew Palmer, Lamyai, Okay_Srisamut. 22–23 – Trum Ronnarong.

CONTENTS

PAGE 4 Go Outside!
PAGE 6 Be Ready!
PAGE 7 Be Kind!
PAGE 8 What Is an Ant?
PAGE 10 Black Garden Ant
PAGE 12 Yellow Meadow Ant
PAGE 14 Wood Ant
PAGE 16 Leafcutter Ant
PAGE 18 Army Ant
PAGE 20 Flying Ant
PAGE 22 Ant Patrol
PAGE 24 Glossary and Index

Words that look like **this** can be found in the glossary on page 24.

GO OUTSIDE!

Outside is a great place to be. It is full of amazing creatures.

Are you ready to learn about them?

You could explore a garden, park, or forest to find creatures.

Look at what is on the pavement!

BE READY!

Make sure you are ready to explore.

You will need:

A snack

Waterproof clothing

Magnifying glass

Backpack

BE KIND!

It is important not to **disturb** any creatures you find.

Leave everything as you found it.

WHAT IS AN ANT?

Ants are a type of **insect**. They live all over the world.

They can be different sizes and colors.

Ants live in all sorts of places, such as fields, woods, and even underground!

Whenever you see a hand, place your thumb on the page to see how big the ant is.

BLACK GARDEN ANT

Actual size

These ants can be found in the garden, under rocks, or even on pavement.

Place your thumb here

These ants leave a smelly trail to let other ants know where to find food.

Queen ants can live for up to 15 years, but some live longer.

YELLOW MEADOW ANT

These ants spend most of their lives underground. They eat **honeydew**.

Actual size

Place your thumb here

Yellow meadow ants create **anthills** in grassy fields.

Yellow meadow anthills

WOOD ANT

Wood ants like to make <u>nests</u> in logs and old tree stumps.

Actual size

Place your thumb here

Wood ants use large piles of pine needles to build their nests.

LEAFCUTTER ANT

These ants use their sharp **jaws** to cut up leaves.

Actual size

Place your thumb here

They can carry things that are up to 50 times heavier than them.

That is like a person carrying a car!

ARMY ANT

Army soldier ant

Actual size

Army ants travel in big groups. They do not nest in one place.

Place your thumb here

Army ants can get across gaps by making a bridge out of themselves.

FLYING ANT

Some places have flying ants. These are ants with wings!

Flying queen ant

Actual size

Place your thumb here

Some flying ants are queen ants looking to make a new nest.

Queen ants are much bigger than other ants.

ANT PATROL

Now that you know more about ants, use these photos to identify the kinds of ants where you live.

Black garden ant

Yellow meadow ant

Wood ant

Leafcutter ant

Army ant

Flying ant

It's time to go... looking for ants!

GLOSSARY

anthills nests made in the shape of a mound or small hill that are built by ants

disturb to move or touch

honeydew a sweet and sticky thing found on parts of some plants

insect an animal that has six legs and sometimes one or two pairs of wings

jaws parts of the mouth that can move

nests places where some animals make their home

queen ants the most important members of their nests and the mothers of all the other ants in a nest

INDEX

anthills 13
exploring 5–6
gardens 5, 10
leaves 16
logs 14
nests 14–15, 18, 21
queen ants 11, 20–21
underground 9, 12